Wait! WHAT?

ALBERT EINSTEIN
Was a Dope?

DAN GUTMAN

illustrated by **ALLISON STEINFELD**

NORTON YOUNG READERS

An Imprint of W. W. Norton & Company
Independent Publishers Since 1923

To kids who like to learn cool stuff.

For information about permission to reproduce selections from this book, write to
Permissions, W. W. Norton & Company, Inc., 500 Fifth Avenue, New York, NY 10110

For information about special discounts for bulk purchases, please contact
W. W. Norton Special Sales at specialsales@wwnorton.com or 800-233-4830

Manufacturing by Sheridan
Book design by Patrick Collins
Production manager: Anna Oler

Library of Congress Cataloging-in-Publication Data

Names: Gutman, Dan, author. | Steinfeld, Allison, illustrator.
Title: Albert Einstein was a dope? / Dan Gutman ; illustrated by Allison Steinfeld.
Description: First edition. | New York, NY : Norton Young Readers, [2021] |
Series: Wait! what? | Audience: Ages 7–10
Identifiers: LCCN 2020051535 | ISBN 9781324015581 (hardcover) |
ISBN 9781324017059 (paperback) | ISBN 9781324015598 (epub) |
ISBN 9781324019428 (kindle edition)
Subjects: LCSH: Einstein, Albert, 1879–1955—Juvenile literature. |
Physicists—Biography—Juvenile literature. | Physicists—Intellectual
life—Juvenile literature.
Classification: LCC QC16.E5 G89 2021 | DDC 530.092 [B]—dc23
LC record available at https://lccn.loc.gov/2020051535

W. W. Norton & Company, Inc.
500 Fifth Avenue, New York, N.Y. 10110
www.wwnorton.com

W. W. Norton & Company Ltd.
15 Carlisle Street, London W1D 3BS

2 4 6 8 0 9 7 5 3 1

CONTENTS

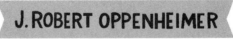

J. ROBERT OPPENHEIMER

Physicist and "Father of the Atomic Bomb"

That's True, But...

I doubt it. I know a lot about Einstein.

 But you don't know this.

 Please excuse my brother. Turner and I have always been interested in famous people. We thought it would be cool to choose some celebrities and learn all about them. But we didn't want to learn regular, boring stuff about famous people that you can find anywhere. We want to learn about unusual stuff. Odd stuff. Strange stuff. Funny stuff.

 Yeah, the stuff you don't see in regular biographies. For instance, did you know that when Albert Einstein died, his brain and eyeballs were removed from his body?

 Wait. What? How do you know that? I didn't come across that in my research. Details!

 I'll tell you all about it later.

 Later? When? What chapter? I want to hear about Einstein's brain and eyeballs right now!

 Sorry, not telling. That's what you get for thinking you're smarter than me.

Not fair! You're mean!

 Be patient, sis. I think we should start this thing off by stating the obvious—Albert Einstein was a dope.

 Turner! He was not!

 It says it right on the cover of this book, so it must be true, right?

 Don't believe everything you read in books. Especially book covers.

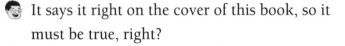

3

Oh yeah? You want facts? When he was a toddler, Albert Einstein had problems learning how to talk. His parents were so worried that they took him to see a doctor.

 So what? He eventually learned how to talk the normal way. That doesn't make him a dope.

 Oh yeah? His family maid called him "the dopey one."

 That's true, but he was at the top of his class in school. He learned geometry on his own, studying over summer vacation. He mastered algebra when he was just twelve, and calculus when he was fifteen.

 True. But he was a high school dropout.

 Well, he got into college anyway.

 Yeah, but when he applied to college, he flunked the sections on literature, zoology, botany, and politics.

 That's also true, but he passed the parts about math and science.

Oh yeah? Well, his college math teacher called him a lazy dog! He even failed physics!

Big deal.

He graduated from college near the bottom of his class. And he wouldn't have graduated at all if he hadn't copied his friend's class notes!

That's all true, but he went on to become a genius! He revolutionized science and the way we look at the world.

I still say he was a dope.

I guess we'll just have to agree to disagree on this one.

Fine. Hey, Did you know it takes five hundred and forty peanuts to make a jar of peanut butter?

What does that have to do with Albert Einstein?

Nothing. I just thought it was a cool true fact.

You're the dope!

CHAPTER 1

Stuff Your Teacher Wants You to Know About Albert Einstein...

1879 He is born on March 14 in Ulm, Germany.

1880 His family moves to Munich, Germany.

1881 Maja, his sister, is born.

1894 The family moves to Milan, Italy. Albert stays in Munich to finish high school.

1895 He drops out of high school and joins his family in Milan. He fails the entrance exam for Zurich Polytechnic, and goes to high school in Switzerland.

1896 He enrolls in the Swiss Federal Institute of Technology.

1902 He gets a job at the patent office in Bern, Switzerland.

1903 He marries Mileva Marić.

1904 Their son Hans Albert is born.

1905 He writes four scientific articles that revolutionize science and he gets his Ph.D. from the University of Zurich.

1909 He quits his job at the patent office and becomes a professor at the University of Zurich.

1910 A second son, Eduard, is born.

1914 Albert and Mileva separate. World War I begins.

1915 He finishes writing his general theory of relativity.

1918 World War I ends.

1919 The theory of relativity is confirmed. He becomes a celebrity. Albert and Mileva divorce. He marries Elsa Löewenthal.

1921 He is awarded the Nobel Prize in physics (but didn't receive it until 1922).

1933 Hitler comes to power in Germany. Albert and Elsa move to the United States and settle in Princeton, New Jersey.

"My life is a simple thing that would interest no one. It is a known fact that I was born, and that is all that is necessary."

9

1936 Elsa Einstein dies.

1939 World War II begins.
He writes a letter to
President Franklin D. Roosevelt
urging him to research nuclear weapons.

1940 He becomes a U.S. citizen.

1941 The United States enters
World War II.

1945 The atomic bomb is dropped on Japan.
World War II ends. Einstein retires.

1948 His first wife, Mileva, dies.

1955 Albert Einstein dies on April 18.

Still awake? Great! Okay, now let's get to the good stuff, the stuff your teacher doesn't even know about Albert Einstein...

10

CHAPTER 2

Baby Einstein

 Okay, let's talk about Einstein's eyeballs and brain, which you said were removed from his body when he died.

11

Albert Einstein wasn't born in a hospital. He was born in his family's home in Ulm, Germany, at eleven-thirty in the morning on Friday, March fourteenth, 1879. The house isn't there anymore.

OTHER STUFF
That Happened on
Einstein's Birthday

 1793   Eli Whitney patents the cotton gin.

 1923   Warren Harding becomes the first president to pay income tax.

 1923   A hockey game is broadcast on radio for the first time.

1950   The FBI puts out its first Ten Most Wanted List.

 1958   Perry Como's "Catch a Falling Star" becomes the first gold record.

1990   Mikhail Gorbachev becomes president of the Soviet Union.

When we think of science geniuses, another name often comes to mind: British astrophysicist Stephen Hawking. As it turned out, Hawking died on Einstein's birthday, and both were the same age when they died—seventy-six.

 Einstein's birthday (3/14) is also "National Pi Day," a yearly celebration of the number (3.14) that represents the ratio of a circle's circumference to its diameter. The holiday began in 1988 and the U.S. House of Representatives recognized it in 2009. Some states hold pie-eating contests to celebrate.

I never knew math was so delicious!

Mhmm!

On Einstein's birthday in 2019, on the International Space Station, Canadian astronaut David Saint-Jacques broadcast a photo of Einstein floating weightlessly, with the earth in the background.

Okay, enough of this birthday stuff! Albert was born with a really big head. His mother thought something was wrong with him.

His parents were planning to name him "Abraham," but they thought it sounded too Jewish. So they kept the *A* and named him "Albert."

Albert's father Hermann was a bed salesman. Later, he got into the field of electrical lighting (a recent invention), and provided light for cities in Germany.

Albert was two years old when his sister Maja was born. He thought she was a toy. When he saw Maja for the first time, he asked his parents, "Where are the wheels?"

Albert and Maja were good friends their whole lives. She was a vegetarian, but she loved hot dogs. When they were young, Einstein told her that hot dogs were a vegetable. She kept eating hot dogs.

When he got mad, Albert's face would turn yellow and he would throw temper tantrums.

When he was five, he got so upset that he threw a chair at his tutor. She quit. Another time, he threw a bowling ball at Maja.

 Other than Maja, Albert didn't have childhood friends. He didn't play with other kids. One family maid called him "Father Bore" because he spent so much time alone. He liked doing puzzles, feeding pigeons, and building houses of cards. Some of them were fourteen stories high.

Instead of asking, "What's for dinner?" or "Why do I have to go to bed so early?" Albert would ask, "What holds the planets in place?" and "Where does the universe end?" Today, Albert Einstein would probably be called a nerd.

Albert was sick in bed one day, and his father bought him a compass. Albert was fascinated by the fact that the needle always pointed north, and was controlled by an invisible force field. It started him wondering why the universe behaved the way it did.

In the 1994 movie *I.Q.*, a character playing Einstein wears the compass around his neck. There's also a 2003 children's book called *Rescuing Einstein's Compass* about a boy who takes Einstein sailing and the compass falls into the lake.

Even though he was Jewish, his parents sent him to Catholic elementary school. He didn't like school. He hated having to memorize things, and complained about it. One teacher announced in front of the class that Albert would never amount to anything.

While he was in high school, Albert's family moved to Italy . . . and they didn't bring him along! The plan was for Albert to finish high school in Germany, but he hated high school too. So he dropped out during Christmas vacation and followed his family to Italy. He didn't tell his parents he was coming. He just showed up! He explained that he would study on his own.

 **"Anything truly novel is invented only during one's youth. Later one becomes more experienced, more famous – and more BLOCKHEADED."**

 Albert applied to a college that didn't require a high school diploma. He got rejected, and had to finish high school in Switzerland.

 Finally, he got into the Swiss Federal Institute of Technology. During college, Albert accidently caused an explosion during a physics class experiment. (Physics is the science of matter and energy and how they interact.) He hurt his right hand badly, and had to get stitches. He couldn't write for two weeks.

> **"** The value of a college education is not the learning of many facts but the **TRAINING OF THE MIND TO THINK. "**

To graduate from college, Albert had to write a research paper. He got one of the lowest grades in the class. Not only that, but he used the wrong kind of paper, so his professor made him copy the whole thing all over again.

We think of Einstein as a funny-looking older guy with hair that looked like he just stuck his finger into an electric socket. But in his younger days, he was good-looking with dark wavy hair and piercing brown eyes. He was five feet eight inches tall.

During his lifetime, Albert Einstein was a citizen of four different countries—Germany, Austria, Switzerland, and the United States—some of them at the same time.

He was a citizen of Switzerland most of his life. All Swiss citizens were required to apply for military service. But Einstein was rejected by the Swiss army.

 Don't tell me—he didn't know how to use a Swiss army knife?

 No, he was rejected because he had varicose veins and sweaty feet!

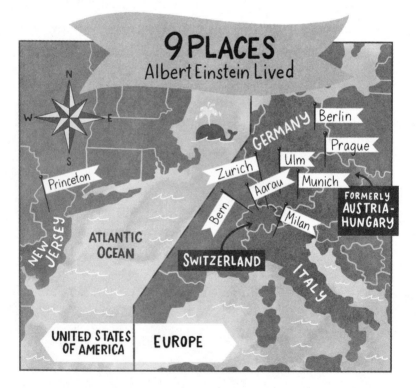

9 PLACES
Albert Einstein Lived

Berlin
Prague
GERMANY
Ulm
Zurich
Aarau
Munich
Princeton
FORMERLY
AUSTRIA-
HUNGARY
Bern
Milan
ATLANTIC
OCEAN
NEW JERSEY
SWITZERLAND
ITALY

UNITED STATES OF AMERICA | EUROPE

N W E S

CHAPTER 3

The "Miracle Year"

 In 1905, Albert Einstein was twenty-six.
He wasn't a professor working at a famous
university. He had a low-level job at the patent
office in Bern, Switzerland. It was an easy job.
Einstein could finish his work in a few hours.
Then he would spend the rest of his time
daydreaming about his own ideas.

"Whenever anybody would come by," he

said, "I would cram my notes into my desk drawer and pretend to work on my office work."

 I do that all the time.

 Yeah, but you're not a genius. Einstein wasn't the kind of scientist who needed a laboratory with test tubes and expensive machines. His "equipment" was paper, a pencil, and his brain.

Ever since he was a teenager, he would do what he called "thought experiments." For

"Anyone who has never made a mistake has never tried anything new."

instance, what would it be like to ride at the speed of light alongside a light beam? If the earth is spinning and we're on a moving train, why do we feel like we're not moving at all? How would gravity be changed if you were trapped in a falling elevator?

WAHOOO

If we were twins and you blasted off in a spaceship at the speed of light while I stayed on earth, would you be younger than me when you came back?

What makes you think I'd come back? But you get the idea. It was these kinds of thought experiments that led Einstein to his "miracle year" of 1905. In four months that year, he would write four scientific papers that would rock the science world.

So let's break 'em down.

1. In March, Einstein wrote a paper about light and the "photoelectric effect." Basically, he said that light comes not just in waves but in tiny particles. (In 1926, they would be named "photons.")

2. In May, he wrote a paper about the random motion ("Brownian motion") of small particles floating in a liquid. Here he proved that atoms and molecules exist, and their sizes can be calculated. Before this, physicists debated whether or not atoms were real.

3. In June, Einstein wrote his most important paper, about his theory of relativity. This was what would make him famous.

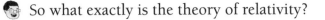 So what exactly is the theory of relativity?

Ha! Relativity is so complicated, even Einstein said he didn't quite grasp it. He once said, "Since the mathematicians have grabbed hold of the theory of relativity, I myself no longer understand it."

One time, a reporter asked him to sum up the theory of relativity, and he replied, "All of my life I have been trying to get it into one book, and he wants me to get it into one sentence!"

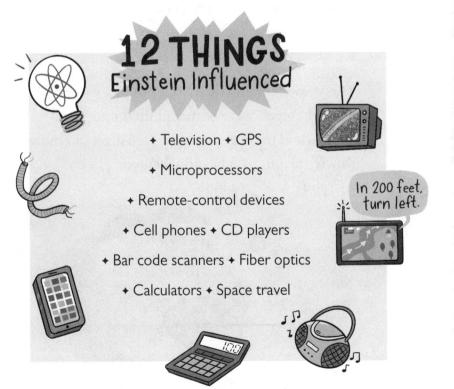

12 THINGS
Einstein Influenced

+ Television + GPS

+ Microprocessors

+ Remote-control devices

+ Cell phones + CD players

+ Bar code scanners + Fiber optics

+ Calculators + Space travel

In 200 feet, turn left.

Einstein got so sick of trying to explain relativity that he came up with the one answer that would shut everybody up: "Pardon me, sorry! Always I am mistaken for Professor Einstein."

Basically, the theory of relativity overturned classic laws of physics that had been around since the time of Isaac Newton. Newton assumed that everything in the universe looked and behaved the same way everywhere. Einstein showed that everything in the universe is moving *relative* to everything else, and things look and behave differently depending on the motion of the observer. Relativity!

This means that if you'd been put in a rocket ship when you were born and fired into space and back at the speed of light, you'd get old more slowly than me. I'd be old when you got back and you'd still be a kid!

Bye brother, I'll see you in 5 minutes when you'll be 100 years old!

$E = mc^2$

 In November 1905, Einstein wrote another paper, and it included the most famous equation in history. You've probably heard of it, even if you don't know what it means. So I'll tell you what it means. The E stands for "energy." The m stands for "mass." Do you know what the c stands for?

Chocolate?

 No, dope! The c stands for the speed of light! Which, by the way, is 186,000 miles per second, or about 670 million miles per hour.

Wow! Light should get a speeding ticket.

So energy equals mass times the square of the speed of light. That may not mean much to us, but to physicists, it helps explain the universe. It means that

Do you know how fast you were going?

mass (stuff like rocks) and energy (like beams of light) are two forms of the same thing!

 So a beam of light and a bag of Doritos are the same thing?

 Uh, not exactly.

 Wait. I actually think I understand Einstein's theory of relativity! Even when I'm sitting on my couch playing video games and eating

"I have no special talents, I am only **PASSIONATELY CURIOUS.**"

Doritos, I'm actually moving about a thousand miles an hour, because that's how fast the earth is spinning at the equator. And while I'm doing that, the earth is moving sixty-seven thousand miles per hour around the sun. The sun gives off light, and I could turn those beams of light into another bag of Doritos!

 Maybe we should move on to the next chapter.

"IMAGINATION IS MORE IMPORTANT THAN KNOWLEDGE. knowledge is limited. Imagination encircles the world."

"If A is success in life, then $A = X + Y + Z$. work is X, play is Y, and Z is keeping your mouth shut."

CHAPTER 4

Getting Famous

 After he shocked the scientific world in 1905, Albert Einstein still wasn't famous. In fact, he couldn't even get a job as a college teacher. In 1908, he applied to be a high school math teacher in Switzerland. Twenty-one people sent in applications. Einstein wasn't even one of the top three finalists. What a loser!

 At one point, Albert's father wrote a letter to a well-known chemistry professor named

Wilhelm Ostwald asking him to hire his son. Ostwald never replied. That must have been humiliating! But nine years later, Ostwald nominated Einstein for the Nobel Prize. So there!

 Finally, four years after he rocked the world of physics, Einstein got hired by the University of Bern in Switzerland. But he kept working at the patent office, because being a junior professor didn't pay enough money to live on.

The problem was, Einstein hadn't invented anything that you could see with your eyes or hold in your hands. Thomas Edison invented the light bulb, which everybody could understand. The Wright Brothers invented the airplane, which everybody could understand.

 Peter Cooper invented Jell-O, which everybody could understand.

 Is that true?

 Look it up.

 Some other time. Most people thought Einstein was just a crackpot with a nutty theory. Only a few scientists in the world understood relativity. And there wasn't even any proof that the theory was right.

The Eclipse

 It turned out there was one way to prove Einstein's theory. Under certain conditions, he predicted, gravity could bend a beam of light.

 What? No way.

Yes way. If you could take a picture of a star where its light passed close to the sun, the position of that star should appear to be slightly different than when its light did not have to pass by the sun—if Einstein's theory was correct. But the only time you could take that picture would be during a solar eclipse, when the starlight would be visible.

For your information, a solar eclipse is when the moon passes right in front of the sun, blocking it out. Even though the sun is much bigger than the moon, both objects look like they're the same size in the sky because the sun is so much farther away. It's an amazing coincidence, really.

Hey, you're blocking my view!

Sorry!

Listen to *you!* Anyway, it just so happened that there was going to be an eclipse in Russia on August twenty-first, 1914. So a team of scientists went there with state-of-the-art telescopes and camera equipment to take pictures of the eclipse. Finally, they would prove

or disprove Einstein's theory. But there was just one problem.

 It was a cloudy day?

No, World War I broke out! The scientists were captured by the Russian army! They thought the scientists were spies.

Gee, I wonder if all those cameras and telescopes had anything to do with it!

It was another five years until the next solar eclipse—May 29, 1919. The eclipse would be sweeping across South America and parts of Africa for six minutes of darkness. So a team of British scientists went to Africa. And this time, they were successful. The clouds opened up just a minute before the total eclipse, and they got the pictures.

The result: The stars were positioned in the photos exactly where Einstein predicted they would be. The theory of relativity had been confirmed.

Rock Star

It took a few months until the proof of Einstein's theory reached the public. In November, the news hit the front page of every newspaper. Radio had recently become popular, and newsreels were in movie theaters. Suddenly Einstein was one of the most famous people in the world. Everyone said he was a genius!

Wherever he went, people went crazy. When Einstein visited New York City, ten thousand people came to see him at City Hall. He was on the cover of *Time* magazine (the first of five times). Parents named their babies Albert.

In the next six years, six hundred books and articles were written about Einstein and his theory. He had become the first scientist to be world-famous in his own lifetime, and one of the first media celebrities to be hounded by photographers and autograph seekers.

 One time, he was taking a train to Vienna, where three thousand people were waiting to hear him speak. When the train arrived, his hosts couldn't find him in the first-class cabin. They looked in the second-class cabin, and Einstein wasn't there either. Finally, they found him in the third-class cabin. He explained that he preferred to travel third-class because fewer people would recognize him and bother him there.

 After a while, being so famous got old. Einstein said that attending a press conference was "like undressing in public."

The Nobel Prize

Einstein was expected to win the Nobel Prize, and he was nominated a bunch of times. But year after year his name was passed over. In 1921, the Nobel Committee for Physics voted to choose *nobody* to win the award rather than give it to Einstein. Many people believed it was because Einstein was Jewish.

 When he finally did win the next year, it wasn't for his theory of relativity. It was for his work on the photoelectric effect. He didn't bother to attend the ceremony. Burn!

Einstein at the Movies

 Albert Einstein didn't become a movie star, but he's been a character in lots of movies and TV shows . . .

LIGHTS, CAMERA, EINSTEIN!

* *The Beginning or the End* (1947)
* *Champagne for Caesar* (1950)
* *Young Einstein* (1988)
* *I.Q.* (1994)
* An Albert Einstein character appears in two episodes of *Star Trek: The Next Generation.*
* In *Back to the Future*, the Doc Brown character looks like Einstein, and his dog is named Einstein.
* In *Star Wars*, Yoda's eyes were modeled after Einstein's eyes.

Beam me up!

We have to save the future!

Betcha Didn't Know...

🧑 Einstein was a fan of movie legend Charlie Chaplin, and they became friends on one of Einstein's trips to America. When Chaplin's movie *City Lights* was first shown in Hollywood, he brought Einstein as his special guest.

🧑 Being so famous, Einstein received plenty of offers to endorse products, but he always turned them down. That has never stopped companies from selling all kinds of stuff with his face on it. Even today, over sixty years after he died, you

can buy Albert Einstein T-shirts, socks, mugs, posters, neckties, jewelry, water bottles, mouse pads, bobblehead dolls, Halloween masks, and talking robot dolls. You can even buy underwear with Albert Einstein's face on it. Don't believe me? Google it.

 The composer Philip Glass created an opera titled *Einstein on the Beach* in 1976. In 1992, Alan Lightman published a best-selling novel called *Einstein's Dreams*. It was made into a musical play in 2019.

At Legoland in Florida, there's a twenty-foot sculpture of Einstein's face made out of Lego blocks.

"Why is it that **NOBODY UNDERSTANDS ME, YET EVERYBODY LIKES ME?**"

"With fame I became more and more **STUPID,** which of course is a very common phenomenon."

In 1996 a Colorado woman was disappointed that there weren't more educational videos for her young daughter. So she made a video in her basement, and titled it *Baby Einstein*. It was a huge success. Five years and lots of videos later, she sold her company to Disney for $25 million.

Just one problem: Studies were done that showed the *Baby Einstein* videos had no educational value. Disney ended up paying out $100 million in refunds, and selling the company.

Albert Einstein would be a world-famous celebrity for the rest of his life, and beyond. In *Time* magazine's final issue of 1999, he was named "Person of the Century."

At one point, Einstein's son Eduard asked his father why he was so famous. Einstein replied, "When a blind beetle crawls over the surface of a curved branch, it doesn't notice that the track it has covered is indeed curved. I was lucky enough to notice what the beetle didn't notice."

 That makes no sense at all.

CHAPTER 5

The Nutty Professor

 Now, about Einstein's eyeballs . . .

Not yet! Besides being a genius, there's another reason why Albert Einstein became so famous. He was funny! Scientists were supposed to be serious, boring people. But Einstein was a ham. He liked cracking jokes, and had a laugh like a barking seal. He was always good for a silly quote. He enjoyed the crowds, photographers, and attention.

Einstein also looked funny. He refused to go to a barber, so his wife Elsa (who was nearsighted) cut his crazy, uncombed hair. He also hated getting dressed up, and refused to go shopping for clothes. So Elsa would take one of his jackets to a clothing store so she could find another one like it that fit.

Mostly, he wore rumpled corduroy pants and cotton sweatshirts. He wore sandals until they had holes in them. He looked sort of like a circus clown.

Oh, and he didn't like wearing socks. When one of his neighbors asked him why he didn't wear them, he replied, "I have reached the age when, if someone tells me to wear socks, I don't have to."

"I am content in my later years. I have kept my good humor and take neither myself nor the next person seriously."

You've probably heard of "the nutty professor" or "the absentminded professor." Einstein was the original absentminded, nutty, scatterbrained professor. He may have been a genius, but he seemed kind of dopey.

Einstein was famous for forgetting things. "I am often so engrossed in my work," he said, "that

I forget to eat lunch." He was always forgetting where he left his keys. When he traveled, he would forget to bring his clothes or his suitcase with him. One time, leaving Zurich, he left behind his nightshirt, umbrella, toothbrush, comb, and hairbrush.

The most amazing part is that Einstein actually had a comb or brush in the first place.

 One time in 1930, Einstein was staying at the fancy Waldorf Astoria Hotel in New York. They gave him two huge suites that were connected to a private dining room. A bunch of guests were visiting him, and at one point somebody noticed that Einstein wasn't around. He had

gotten lost in his own hotel room! Finally, he
had the hotel close off one of the suites to make
it easier for him to find his way around.

Einstein once received a check
for $1,500. Instead of cashing
it, he used it as a bookmark.
Then he lost the book and couldn't
remember who sent him the check.
Eventually, his wife figured it out and
got a replacement.

One day, Einstein was looking for a paper clip in
his office. He found one, but it was bent. While
he was looking for a tool to straighten out the

paper clip, he came across a box of new paper clips. Instead of just using one of the new paper clips in the box, he made a tool out of one so he could straighten the bent paper clip.

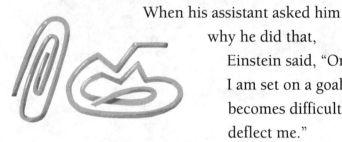

When his assistant asked him why he did that, Einstein said, "Once I am set on a goal, it becomes difficult to deflect me."

Here's the best story: One day a man called the university where Einstein was working and asked for his home address. When the secretary told the caller she couldn't give out that personal information, the man on the phone admitted that he was Einstein himself. "I'm on my way home," he told her, "and I've forgotten where my house is."

CHAPTER 6

Albert Einstein— Ladies' Man!

 Women were crazy about Einstein. That hair! Those clothes! The muscles in his brain!

It's not a joke. Einstein attracted lots of women—but he wasn't always so nice to them. Here are a few that were a part of his life . . .

Marie Winteler

 Einstein's first girlfriend. He lived with her family during high school when his parents moved to Italy. The relationship didn't last long, but even after he moved away, he would mail Marie his dirty laundry to wash it. Then she would mail it back to him. So romantic! Einstein eventually broke up with Marie by writing a letter to her mother.

Betcha Didn't Know…

 Marie's brother Paul got married to Einstein's sister Maja, and Maja's daughter Anna got married to Einstein's best friend Michele Besso.

Mileva Marić

Einstein's first wife. They met in college. She was a physics student from Serbia, and the only girl in the class.

In one of her letters to him, she wrote, "Oh, it was really neat at the lecture of Professor Lenard yesterday. He is talking now about the kinetic theory of heat and gases." You can see why they were meant for each other.

Albert nicknamed Mileva "Dollie" and she nicknamed him "Johnnie." He wrote her this poem . . .

Oh my! That Johnnie Boy!
So crazy with desire.
While thinking of his Dollie.
His pillow catches fire.

XO Albert

Maybe it sounded better in German. Anyway, Albert's mother Pauline didn't like Mileva, partly because she was three years older than he was. When Albert told his mom he was going to marry Mileva, she threw herself on a bed, buried her head in a pillow, and cried. "You are ruining your future."

 Albert and Mileva got married in 1903, and neither of their families came to the wedding. They had little money, so they didn't have a honeymoon.

 Albert and Mileva were happy, for a while. She helped him check the math in his papers. Some people even believe Mileva deserved to be called the theory of relativity's coauthor.

But it must have been hard to live with such a famous and eccentric man. Mileva became gloomy, depressed, and she suffered from rheumatism. After having two sons (more about them later), Albert and Mileva separated in 1914. Albert wanted to get a divorce, but Mileva refused. So he drew up a contract and made a list of demands if they were to stay married...

EINSTEIN'S DEMANDS

+ Mileva had to wash his clothes.

+ She had to give him three meals a day in his room.

+ She would tidy up his bedroom.

+ He would not have to sit at home with her.

+ She could not travel with him.

+ She would leave the room as soon as he told her to.

+ She would not make fun of him in front of the children.

+ She would stop talking to him if he asked her to.

He sounds a little like a jerk, to me.

 Yeah, maybe Einstein thought Mileva would never agree to those demands and just give him a divorce. But she said okay!

 So Einstein made another offer to Mileva. He said that if she divorced him and he won the Nobel Prize, he would give her the prize money. She agreed to that in 1919, and surprise, surprise, he won the Nobel Prize three years later. Mileva used the money (about thirty-two thousand dollars) to buy three apartments in Zurich, which she rented out.

When she died in 1948, eighty-five thousand Swiss francs were found under Mileva's mattress.

 One reason why Einstein wanted a divorce was because he had met somebody else . . .

Elsa Einstein

 Einstein's second wife. She was also his first cousin. Four months after his divorce was final, Albert married Elsa.

Albert and Elsa had played together when they were kids. Like Mileva, Elsa was three years older.

She didn't mind being married to such a famous man. In fact, she enjoyed it. When people crowded around Albert, Elsa would charge them a dollar for an autograph and five dollars if they wanted to have their pictures taken with him. Then she donated the money to charities for children.

As well as German, Elsa spoke English and

French, so she served as Albert's translator. She took care of him, packing his suitcase for trips and giving him pocket money when he needed cash. (He usually didn't carry any.) She even told him when to eat. When he said he was too busy with his research to stop for a meal, Elsa would tell him, "People have centuries to find things out, but your stomach, no, it will not wait for centuries."

Elsa had poor eyesight, but she didn't think she looked good in glasses, so she refused to wear them. Sometimes she bumped into furniture while walking around. One time she

"Well, my husband does that on the back of an old envelope."

ELSA EINSTEIN

After being shown a telescope that could help determine the size of the universe.

was at a fancy dinner and there was a decorative orchid flower on her plate. She thought it was her salad and started cutting it up.

Elsa died from heart and kidney problems in 1936.

 After Elsa died, Einstein received marriage proposals from numerous women. But even while Elsa was alive, Einstein had relationships with a number of women. One of them was a Russian spy. More on her later.

Einstein's kids

Albert Einstein had three children with his first wife . . .

Hans Albert Einstein was born in 1904. When he told his dad that he wanted to become an engineer, Einstein replied, "I think it's a disgusting idea." Hans Albert did it anyway and became a respected expert in hydraulics.

Father and son had an on-and-off relationship for many years, but became close as Einstein got older. Hans Albert died in 1973. He had two sons and five grandchildren, so there are some great-grandchildren of Albert Einstein's running around today.

Eduard Einstein was born in 1910. He played piano, enjoyed poetry, and studied medicine in college. But most of his life he was sick, both physically and mentally. He was diagnosed with schizophrenia and spent years in what used to be called an insane asylum. He died in 1965.

Lieserl (short for Elizabeth) Einstein was Einstein's first child, born in 1902. But it wasn't until 1986—when some letters between Albert and Mileva were found—that anybody even knew that Lieserl existed.

What we know is that Lieserl caught scarlet fever when she was a baby. Einstein was out of the country when she was born, and he probably never met her. Albert and Mileva never

"Enjoying the joys of others and suffering with them—these are the best guides for man."

told their parents or friends about Lieserl. She was most likely put up for adoption and died as a toddler, but nobody knows for sure.

In the 1930s, a woman claimed to be Einstein's daughter. She wasn't.

Was Einstein a good father? Yes and no. When he was deep in his work—which was most of the time—he neglected his family. And often he lived in a different country from Mileva and the boys. But he did support and care for Hans Albert and Eduard. One of the few times Albert Einstein cried was when he and Mileva separated in 1914 and she took the boys with her.

CHAPTER 7

Einstein in His Spare Time

 I think it's about time we get into the issue of Einstein's brain and eyeballs.

What's your rush? There's other stuff we need to talk about first. Albert Einstein didn't spend his whole life sitting around thinking about the universe. He also spent a lot of time on his hobbies. Like...

Music

Einstein's mother played piano, and she had him take violin lessons when he was a little boy. He played violin his whole life, until the last few years when he switched to piano because it became too difficult to move his fingers.

"If I were not a physicist, I would probably be a musician. I live my daydreams in music."

"I get the most joy in life out of music."

He loved Mozart, Bach, and Schubert, but there was one composer he didn't like. "I feel uncomfortable listening to Beethoven," Einstein said.

Playing violin relaxed Einstein, and also helped him think. Often he would be working on a complicated problem and take a break to play his violin. After playing for a few minutes, he would suddenly exclaim, "That's it, now I have it!"

He liked to play music in his kitchen because the sound bounced off the walls in there. He named his violin "Lina." He took it with him everywhere he went and would start playing with anyone who had an instrument. One time he was playing with the famous violinist Fritz Kreisler and fell

I've got it !!!

out of rhythm. Kreisler said, "What's the matter, Professor, can't you count?"

Some people said Einstein was pretty good. But others said he was "pathetic" and, "He bowed like a lumberjack."

That's not fair! I bet there are some lumberjacks who are great violinists.

63

✦ Einstein's face is one of many celebrities on the cover of the album *Sgt. Pepper's Lonely Hearts Club Band* by the Beatles.

✦ There's a song titled "Einstein" on Kelly Clarkson's album *Stronger*.

✦ Mariah Carey had an album titled $E = MC^2$.

✦ To celebrate the news that his theory of relativity had been proven, Einstein bought himself a new violin.

Sailing

Einstein loved to sail, and would go out sailing by himself—which was probably not a good idea because he refused to wear a life jacket and he didn't know how to swim. His family and friends would get very worried if he was late coming home.

For his fiftieth birthday, some friends bought him a twenty-three-foot sailboat. He designed it himself and named it *Tummler* which means "dolphin." Later, he got another sailboat he called *Tinef*, which is a Yiddish word that means "a piece of junk."

Inventions

Inventing things ran in the Einstein family. Albert's uncle Jakob was an inventor who received patents for arc lamps, circuit breakers, and electric meters. And Einstein's first job was working at the Swiss patent office evaluating other people's inventions.

Although he was famous for his theories about light, time, motion, and gravity, Einstein also patented some actual inventions. The strangest one was for an expandable suit jacket for men. Yes, it's true! He invented it in 1936.

 How do you make an expandable jacket?

Simple. You put on two sets of buttons! So when the guy gains weight and his waistline gets bigger, he can just switch to the second set of buttons. Genius!

Einstein's other inventions were more serious. He patented a sound recorder, a navigational gyroscope, a machine that could amplify and measure electricity, and a camera that automatically adjusted the amount of light that came through the lens.

In the 1920s, a refrigerator in Berlin leaked toxic fumes and killed a family. So Einstein and a Hungarian physicist, Leo Szilard, teamed up to invent a safer refrigerator that was noiseless and had no moving parts. But it was never marketed.

Leo Szilard also cowrote a famous letter that Einstein sent to President Franklin Roosevelt. You can read about that in the next chapter.

Altogether, Einstein held about fifty patents, but none of them were successful. He was better at figuring out the universe than he was at building machines.

CHAPTER 8

Einstein
and the Bomb

 Albert Einstein was a lifelong pacifist, which means he was opposed to war or violence as a way to settle disputes. He always tried to avoid conflict. He didn't even like to play chess or Monopoly.

But then came Adolph Hitler and the Nazis.

 Yeah. Einstein had been living peacefully in Berlin for seventeen years. During that time, the Nazis took control of the German government. They were violently anti-Semitic, which means they hated Jewish people. Many German scientists—including Einstein—were Jewish. Their lives were in danger.

The Nazis were just gaining power in 1932, when they declared Albert Einstein to be an enemy of the state. His books were burned and his bank accounts were frozen. His apartment was raided five times. The Nazis even seized his sailboat, claiming it could be used for smuggling. There were threats against his life.

When he heard the Nazis had put a five-thousand-dollar price on his head, Einstein said, "I didn't know it was worth that much!"

But he knew it was serious. It was time for him to leave Germany. That December, he and his wife Elsa got on a train to Belgium with thirty pieces of luggage. From there they sailed to the United States.

Elsa's daughter Margot managed to get Einstein's important papers to the French embassy. She would get out of Germany too, but not all of Einstein's relatives escaped. His cousin Roberto's wife and two daughters were killed by the Nazis and their house was burned down. Roberto later committed suicide.

 During the 1930s, it became obvious that the Nazis were preparing for war, and Einstein realized that pacifism wasn't going to stop them.

In the spring of 1939, an old friend—Danish physicist Niels Bohr—came to visit Einstein in America. Bohr told him that German scientists had figured out how to split the atom (that is, break up the nucleus) by bombarding uranium with neutrons. Both men knew this could lead to an explosive nuclear chain reaction—an atomic bomb.

 Einstein decided that he had to do something. If the Nazis could build atomic bombs, they could take over the world. In August, he sat down with Hungarian physicist Leo Szilard (yes, the refrigerator guy) and wrote a letter to President Roosevelt. This is an excerpt from that letter . . .

> *The element uranium may be turned into a new and important source of energy in the immediate future...It may become possible to set up a nuclear chain reaction in a large mass of uranium... This new phenomena would also lead to the construction of bombs, and it is conceivable—though much less certain— that extremely powerful bombs of a new type may thus be constructed.*

The letter ended with a warning that German scientists might be working on an atomic bomb. A month later, Germany invaded Poland and World War II began.

The United States wasn't in the war yet, but President Roosevelt didn't hesitate. "This requires action," he said. The United States started a top-secret program—the Manhattan Project—to create an atomic bomb before the Nazis could build one.

A number of Germany's Jewish scientists had fled the country to escape the Nazis. Niels Bohr was half Jewish. When the Nazis took over Denmark, Bohr and his son escaped in a small boat to Sweden. He got a fake passport and came to America.

Hitler didn't seem to care. "If the dismissal of Jewish scientists means the annihilation of contemporary German science," he said, "then we shall do without science for a few years!"

What a dumb move. If the Nazis had built the atomic bomb first, they might have won the war.

Most people don't know this, but Einstein wrote a *second* letter to President Roosevelt. It was March 1945, and it was obvious that Germany was about to be defeated. They didn't have a bomb. America was still at war with Japan, and it didn't look like the Japanese were going to surrender.

Einstein (and other scientists) were worried that the United States would use the atomic bomb, kill thousands of innocent people, and begin a new kind of horrible warfare. After all, it would only be a matter of time before other countries figured out how to make atomic weapons. Einstein wrote a letter to President Roosevelt with his concerns.

 What did Roosevelt do that time?

Nothing. He never read the letter. He died on April twelfth, 1945, and Einstein's letter was found in his office.

Four months later, the next president, Harry Truman, gave the okay to drop atomic bombs on the Japanese cities Hiroshima and Nagasaki. An estimated hundred and eighty-five thousand people died. But as a result, World War II was over, and an invasion of Japan (which also would have killed many thousands of people) was avoided.

Albert Einstein didn't invent the atomic bomb. He just warned the president that Germany might be working on one. But it didn't matter. Whether Einstein liked it or not, he came to be called the "father of the atomic bomb." *Time* magazine put him on the cover again, this time with a mushroom cloud and the equation $E = mc^2$

on it. Newsweek used the headline "The Man Who Started It All."

Einstein felt terrible. He had written that first letter to prevent Germany from getting the bomb, not to kill innocent Japanese people. Later, he told a friend his biggest regret was writing that first letter to President Roosevelt.

He said that if he'd known the Germans would not have been able to build a bomb, "I never would have lifted a finger."

He spent the rest of his life speaking out against nuclear warfare and campaigning for all the nations of the world to start an organization that would prevent wars.

 After World War II was over and Einstein was an old man, he said, "I would rather choose to be a plumber."

Naturally, he was given an honorary membership card from the Plumbers and Steamfitters Union.

Whoops!

Betcha Didn't Know...

Even though he wasn't involved in building the atomic bomb, Einstein was part of the war effort. He was paid twenty-five dollars per day as a consultant helping to figure out the best way to place mines in Japanese harbors. "I am in the Navy," he said, "but not required to get a Navy haircut."

Einstein also donated a copy of his relativity paper to be auctioned off and raise money to fight the war. It sold for over eleven million dollars.

In 1952, after the first hydrogen bomb was tested on an island in the Pacific, scientists discovered a new atomic element in the debris. It was named "Einsteinium."

$11,000,000.00 + TAX

THEORY OF RELATIVITY
BY:
ALBERT EINSTEIN

CHAPTER 9

Einstein's Later Life

 When he left Germany at the end of 1932, Einstein got job offers from universities all over the world. He had visited the United States twice before, and liked the freedom and democracy he found there.

Plus, he was treated like a rock star.

Right. He decided to accept a position at the Institute for Advanced Study in Princeton, New Jersey. Einstein lived in Princeton for the rest of his life, and he became a U.S. citizen in 1940. He never went back to Europe .

These days, it's not so easy for immigrants to come and live in the United States. But it helps if you have a special EB-1 visa, which is nicknamed an "Einstein visa." It's reserved for immigrants with "extraordinary ability." That often means they've won the Nobel Prize, or an Oscar, or an Olympic medal.

Do you know the first thing Einstein did when he arrived in Princeton?

He bought a newspaper and an ice-cream cone?

Yes! How did you know that?

The same way you did. I looked it up.

The Institute for Advanced Study agreed to pay Einstein ten thousand dollars a year. That was pretty good money in 1933. But when word

got out that another scientist at the institute was getting paid fifteen thousand, Einstein was given a raise to match it.

Einstein was a simple man. On his first day of work at Princeton, he was asked what equipment he needed for his office. All he wanted was a desk, a chair, pencils, paper, and a large garbage can "so I can throw away all my mistakes."

His whole life, Einstein loved walking and hiking. It wasn't unusual to see him, one of the most famous men in the world, strolling down the street in Princeton. One time a driver spotted him and was so distracted that he drove his car into a tree.

To the kids of Princeton, Einstein wasn't a famous celebrity. He was just a funny-looking old guy with crazy hair. When trick-or-treaters rang his doorbell on that first Halloween in America, Einstein took out his violin and serenaded them.

One day, an eight-year-old girl named Adelaide walked up to Einstein's door, rang the bell, and asked him if he would help her with her math homework. She even brought him fudge! You would think the great man might have told her to get lost. But you know what he did instead?

He invited her inside and helped her with her homework?

Yes! Not only that, but Adelaide kept coming back again and again. When her parents found out Einstein was helping her with her homework, they were mortified and they apologized to him.

"She was a very naughty girl," he told them. "Do you know she tried to bribe me with candy?"

Kids Say the Darndest Things to Einstein

 People wrote letters to Einstein, and he would often answer them. One man wrote saying that he believed gravity and the rotation of the earth turned people upside down and made them do silly things like fall in love. Einstein wrote back, "Falling in love is not the most stupid thing that people do, but gravitation cannot be held responsible for it."

The best letters to Einstein came from kids. Here are three of them...

Dear Mr. Einstein,

I am a little girl of six. I saw your picture in the paper. I think you ought to have a haircut, so you can look better.

Cordially yours,
Ann

Dear Mr. Einstein,

I am writing to you to find out if you really exist. You may think this very strange, but some pupils in our class thought you were a comic strip character.

Yours sincerely,
June

Dear Dr. Einstein,

*My Father and I are going to build a
rocket and go to Mars or Venus. We
hope you will go too. We want you to
go because we need a good scientist and
someone who can guide a rocket good.
Do you care if Mary goes too? She is
two years old. She is a very nice girl.
Everybody has to pay for his food because
we will go broke if we pay!*

*Love,
John*

Betcha Didn't Know...

Einstein could have become the president
of Israel! When the country's first president,
Chaim Weizmann, died in 1952, Einstein was
approached about taking the job. He turned it
down, saying, "I am not the person for that and
I cannot possibly do it."

Einstein suffered from stomach pains much of his life. Back in 1917, he got so sick that he lost fifty pounds in two months.

By the 1950s, he was in his seventies and slowing down. His scientific achievements were far behind him. He was coming to the end of his life and he knew it. When Einstein was asked if he believed in immortality, he said, "No. And one life is enough for me."

Albert Einstein died on Monday, April eighteenth, 1955. The cause of death was an abdominal aneurysm, which is when an artery becomes enlarged. An operation might have prolonged his life, but he refused to have one. The artery burst, and that was that.

The Mystery of Einstein's Last Words

Einstein grew up speaking German, and that was the only language that he spoke fluently. He also spoke some French, and picked up a little English when he lived in Princeton at the end of his life. But according to one colleague, he only knew three hundred English words.

"I am learning English," Einstein said, "but it doesn't want to stay in my old brain."

Just before he died at one o'clock in the morning, he spoke a few words to the nurse who was taking care of him. But he said them in German, and the nurse didn't speak German. So we'll never know Einstein's last words.

Einstein's Brain!

Well it's about time!

Okay, okay. I'll tell you everything. And this is all true.

 I'm listening.

Einstein didn't want his body to be buried, or have a grave site where people would come and pay their respects to him. His body was cremated and his ashes were scattered near Princeton in the Delaware River. But two parts of his body weren't cremated. First, his brain. You'd better sit down for this.

I'm on the edge of my seat.

Okay, there have been lots of rumors about what happened to Einstein's brain after he died. Some people said it was going to be cloned, auctioned off, sent on a world tour, or shot into outer space.

So what really happened to it?

The doctor at Princeton Hospital who did the autopsy on Einstein was named Thomas Harvey. He decided that it would be a good idea to save Einstein's brain so future researchers could study it. He claimed that he got permission from Einstein's son Hans Albert, but that was never confirmed. Anyway, Dr. Harvey just kept the brain himself. It was 2.64 pounds, by the way.

What? You can take somebody's brain and keep it? What did he do with it?

He cut it in half, put it in two cookie jars, and stored them in the corner of his office behind a picnic cooler.

You are kidding me!

No! And sometimes Dr. Harvey kept the brain in a cider box behind a beer cooler.

 No way!

 Yes way! And he held on to Einstein's brain for over forty years. Every so often, Dr. Harvey would cut pieces of the brain off and send them to researchers around the world to examine. He wanted to know if there was something about Einstein's brain that was different from a normal brain and made him a genius.

 Unbelievable!

But it's all true. Dr. Harvey moved a few times, and he would always take Einstein's brain with him. When he was eighty-four years old, he drove to California with the brain in the trunk of a Buick Skylark. He kept it in a Tupperware container inside a duffel bag.

 My head is spinning.

 When he got to California, he gave the brain to

Einstein's granddaughter, Evelyn. But she didn't want it. So he took it back and two years later, when he was eighty-six, Dr. Harvey brought the brain back to Princeton Hospital. Harvey died in 2007. He was ninety-four.

 So what if I wanted to see Einstein's brain today?

 There are pieces of it at the University Medical Center of Princeton, the National Museum of Health and Medicine in Silver Spring, Maryland, and the Mütter Museum in Philadelphia.

 Talk about scatterbrained!

 But you don't have to go *anywhere* to see Einstein's brain. You can see it in the comfort of your living room, for just ninety-nine cents. There's a smartphone app called the Einstein Brain Atlas that contains three hundred and fifty images.

 And what about his eyeballs?

 I'm going to save that for the last chapter.

 Noooooooo!

CHAPTER 10

Oh Yeah? (Stuff About Einstein That Didn't Fit Anywhere Else)

 The first scientific paper Einstein published was about water clinging to the inside of a straw. It's called the "capillary effect." He was just twenty-two years old when he wrote it. Later, he called that paper "worthless."

 Einstein didn't drink alcohol, and called beer "a recipe for stupidity." He would have liked

Einstein's
FAVORITE FOODS

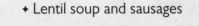

✦ Lentil soup and sausages

✦ Strawberries with whipped cream

✦ Lamb chops and string beans

✦ Honey
(he would buy it by the bucketful)

✦ Eggs (two every morning)
with mushrooms

✦ Egg drop soup

✦ Salmon with mayonnaise

✦ Macaroni

✦ Black tea

✦ Celery punch

to have been a vegetarian, but because of his stomach problems, doctors advised him to eat meat. He ate steak, but only if it was well done.

In his seventies, his doctor instructed him to stop eating meat. He wrote: "I am living without fats, without meat, without fish, but am feeling quite well this way."

Einstein was not one of those geniuses like Thomas Edison who only slept a few hours each night. He got ten hours of sleep, and he also took naps.

This is the one story in this book that may or may not be true: He would nap in a chair while holding a spoon in his hand and a metal plate underneath it. When he dropped the spoon it hit the plate, and the noise let him know it was time to wake up. Or that's the legend, anyway.

Einstein slept in the nude. As he put it, "I sleep as nature made me."

He had no problem with nudity. On one of his first trips to America, he sunbathed nude in the Mojave Desert. And it was not unusual for him to walk around naked in front of his employees or relatives. His housekeeper Herta Waldow wrote, "Either Herr Professor had not bothered putting on his bathrobe, or he was too lost in thought to remember to wear it."

Einstein smoked a pipe, and his wife Elsa was not happy about it. One Thanksgiving he made a bet with her that he could stop smoking for the rest of the year. He won the bet, but when he woke up in the morning on January first, he lit up his pipe.

Toward the end of his life, Einstein gave up smoking entirely, on doctor's orders.

Einstein was a supporter of civil rights. In 1937, the singer Marian Anderson had a concert in Princeton, but a local hotel wouldn't let her stay there because she was African American. So Einstein invited Anderson to stay at his house. They became friends, and after that she stayed at Einstein's house whenever she was in Princeton.

Einstein kept pictures of four people on the wall over his desk...

✦ Sir Isaac Newton, the English mathematician and astronomer

✦ English scientist Michael Faraday

✦ Scottish scientist James Clerk Maxwell

✦ Mahatma Gandhi, the Indian politician
and social activist

 The personal computer didn't exist in Einstein's time. But he didn't even use a typewriter. He wrote everything by hand.

Einstein's PETS

+ A parakeet named Bibo
+ Cats named Tiger and Peter
+ A white terrier named Chico
+ Goldfish

CHEW CHEW

Because he was foreign, famous, outspoken, and associated with some controversial organizations, the FBI kept a close watch on Einstein for years. During his life, they collected 1,427 pages of documents about him. They were stored in fourteen boxes.

But there was one secret the FBI never discovered. Toward the end of his life, Einstein dated a woman named Margarita Konenkova, who turned out to be a Russian spy! Nobody knew about it until over forty years after Einstein died, when nine love letters he wrote to Konenkova became public.

Einstein didn't drive. His wife said it would be too complicated for him.

One time, he was being driven around in a convertible when it started raining. Einstein took off his hat and put it under his coat. His driver asked why he did that, and he replied, "My hair has withstood water many times before, but I don't know how many times my hat can."

On one trip to California, Einstein was filmed behind the wheel of a parked car, and a special effects team made it look as though he was driving around Los Angeles, up into the sky, and over the Rocky Mountains.

Einstein's Eyeballs!

 Okay, tell me everything!

 Well, it just so happens that when Dr. Harvey did the autopsy on Einstein and removed his brain, he also removed Einstein's eyeballs.

 Well, of course. That makes sense. And what did he do with them?

He gave them to Einstein's eye doctor, Henry Abrams.

 What! Why?

 They were friends. I guess he thought Einstein's eyeballs would be a nice gift.

"Having his eyes means the professor's life has not ended," Dr. Abrams said. "A part of him is still with me."

Sure, that makes sense. Body parts make great gifts.

Dr. Abrams died in 2009. He kept Einstein's eyeballs in a safe-deposit box in New York City. And that's where they are today.

That's it. I'm outta here. Now I know more than I need to know about Albert Einstein.

TO FIND OUT MORE . . .

 Have we got you interested in the life of Albert Einstein? Great! There are lots of other books for kids about him.

Ask if your librarian has some of these...

+ *Genius: A Photobiography of Albert Einstein* by Marfe Ferguson Delano (2008)

+ *Albert Einstein* by Kathleen Krull and Boris Kulikov (2015)

+ *Albert Einstein: A Biography* by Milton Meltzer (2007)

- *Albert Einstein: Genius of the Twentieth Century* by Allison Lassieur (2005)

- *Who Was Albert Einstein?* by Jess Braillier (2002)

- *Albert Einstein: A Life of Genius* by Elizabeth MacLeod (2003)

- *Albert Einstein* by Chris Oxlade (2003)

- *Albert Einstein* by Lola Schaefer and Wyatt Schaefer (2003)

- *The Importance of Albert Einstein* by Clarice Swisher (1994)

EINSTEIN ARCHIVES:

http://www.alberteinstein.info/gallery/gallery.html

ACKNOWLEDGMENTS

Thanks to Kristin Allard, Simon Boughton, Allison Steinfeld, Liza Voges, Nina Wallace, and especially Walter Isaacson. I didn't dig into the Einstein archives and go through thousands of pages of documents. Isaacson did. I read lots of books about Einstein, but most of them seem to have gotten their information from Isaacson's best-selling biography, *Einstein: His Life and Universe*. For that, I am deeply grateful.

ABOUT THE AUTHOR

Dan Gutman has written many books for young readers, such as: My Weird School, The Genius Files, Flashback Four, *The Kid Who Ran for President*, *The Homework Machine*, *The Million Dollar Shot*, and the Baseball Card Adventure series. Dan and his wife Nina live New York City. You can find out more about Dan and his books by visiting his website (www.dangutman.com) or following him on Facebook, Twitter, or Instagram.

TITLES IN THE

Wait! WHAT?

SERIES